PARABLES OF JESUS

Rose Visual Bible Studies

Parables of Jesus
Rose Visual Bible Studies

Published by Rose Publishing
An imprint of Tyndale House Ministries
Carol Stream, Illinois
rose-publishing.com

ISBN 979-8-4005-0342-9

Author: Mike Nappa, MA in Bible and Theology, Calvin Theological Seminary; BA in Christian Education, Biola University; author of the award-winning commentary *Bible-Smart: Matthew*

Printed in the United States of America
May 2025, 1st printing

Contents

He never taught without using parables.

Mark 4:34

Parables of Jesus

Here is a quick quiz for you: *How many parables of Jesus are recorded in the New Testament? Your choices: (a) 33, (b) 37, (c) 39, (d) 59, (e) 71, or (f) 79.*

If you chose any of these answers, you're probably correct, since there is no single, unifying description of exactly what a parable is. With so many definitions in play, teachers have applied a wide range of meanings, from the simple to the complex. For instance,

- "A pithy saying" or "extended story" that "teaches a spiritual lesson by illustrating the point with images from everyday life"[1]
- "An expanded analogy"[2]
- "Proverb," "picturesque and suggestive speech," "figurative discourse," "allegory," and "wayside saying."[3]

Well, you get the idea. And while it may be true that we don't know exactly *what* a parable is, and we can't say for sure *how many* parables Jesus taught, here is what we do know:

1. The original Greek word implies a comparison. The word used in the New Testament is *parabole*, which is comprised of two words: *para*, meaning "beside," and *ballo*, "to cast." Thus, a parable is a comparison between two things by *casting* (setting) one thing *beside* another. This is most likely why Jesus often began a parable with a comparison statement such as "The Kingdom of Heaven *is like* ..."

2. Jesus didn't invent the parable. Contrary to popular belief, Jesus used an already-popular form of teaching when he spoke in parables. Others who taught in parables include Plato and Aristotle and the Old Testament prophets Nathan and Isaiah (2 Sam. 12:1–25; Isa. 5:1–7). Even Jewish rabbis living prior to and during the lifetime of Jesus taught using parables.

3. Jesus's parables are often grouped into specific categories. In this study, we'll dig into key parables within five categories: (1) God's nature, (2) judgment, (3) redemption, (4) right living, and (5) God's kingdom. But note that often a parable can overlap several categories. For example, the Parable of the Lost Sheep (Luke 15:3–7) is categorized as a parable of redemption in session 4, but it also clearly reveals God's nature.

To begin our study, let's consider the question, *Why did Jesus choose parables as his primary method for communicating truth to our world?* For the answer, turn the page and dive into session 1: "Why Parables?"

1 WHY PARABLES?

The Disciples Question Jesus

Why Parables?

One thing that is appealing about Jesus's disciples is that they tended to ask Jesus questions that we might be too afraid to ask God ourselves. In Matthew 13:1–9, Jesus tells a large crowd of people his now-famous Parable of the Farmer Scattering Seed (often called the Parable of the Sower) ... and the disciples don't get it.

Confused, the disciples ask Jesus privately, "Why do you use parables when you talk to the people?" (Matt. 13:10). Jesus's answer is a little surprising: "This fulfills the prophecy of Isaiah that says, 'When you hear what I say, you will not understand. When you see what I do, you will not comprehend'" (Matt. 13:14).

Was Jesus deliberately trying to confuse his hearers and hide the truth of God from them? That would seem unexpected and confusing. In this session, then, let's take some time to explore this Matthew 13 moment a little more deeply.

Read It

Key Bible Passage

For this session, read Matthew 13:10–17.

Optional Reading

Explore Mark 4:10–12 and Luke 8:9–10 to see how the other Gospel writers described this same moment in history.

Blessed are your eyes, because they see; and your ears, because they hear.

MATTHEW 13:16

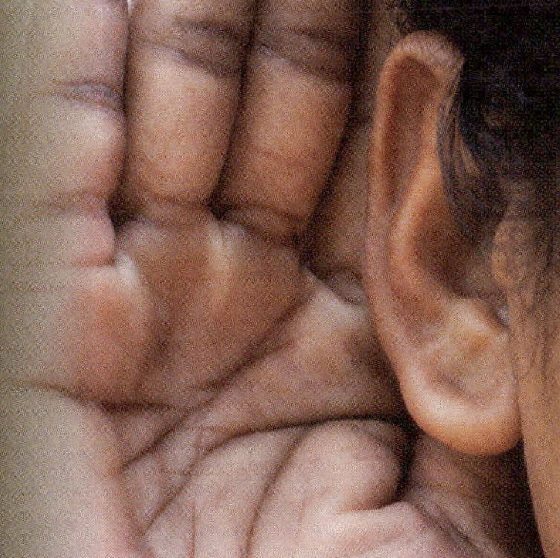

1. What does Jesus say are the consequences for those who listen to his teachings and for those who do not?

   - ❑ Consequences for those who listen: ______________________
     ____

   - ❑ Consequences for those who don't listen: ________________
     ____

2. What are some reasons why people may choose not to listen?

3. If you had been present when Jesus explained his purpose for parables, what follow-up questions would you have wanted to ask?

Key Words from Matthew 13:10–17

ENGLISH WORD (NLT)	GREEK ROOT WORD	MEANING
"permitted" (v. 11)	*didomi*	To grant, or to bestow as a gift; to give one something, to his advantage
"secrets" (v. 11)	*musterion*	Mysteries, as in "some element of God's plan which was not revealed in the Old Testament, but which is revealed in the New"[4]
"hear" (vv. 13–17)	*akouo*	Emphasizes the act of hearing, as well as analyzing and implementing what was heard
"understand" (vv. 13–15)	*suniemi*	To put together mentally; to comprehend and be wise, with the implication of acting well as a result
"hardened" (v. 15)	*pachuno*	To make thick; to fatten; to dull

The Shift to Parables

Up to this point in his ministry, Jesus had most often spoken plainly about his purpose and the things of heaven. His exorcisms and miracles of healing and provision were also straightforward in communicating his identity as the Jewish Messiah and Son of God. Then, rather suddenly, he switched his teaching methodology by placing heavy emphasis on ambiguous stories—parables that he never explained to his wider audiences, and only rarely to his inner circle of disciples. The shift was important enough that three of the four Gospel writers recorded the moment for history, and it was apparently dramatic enough for Christ's disciples to notice it—and to question it: "Why do you use parables when you talk to the people?" (Matt. 13:10). Jesus answered, "*You are permitted to understand the secrets of the Kingdom of Heaven, but others are not*" (Matt. 13:11). This is the beginning of what is known as a "hard saying" of Jesus—something he said that is difficult to accept or seems at odds with other tenets of Scripture. In slightly varied forms, the full hard saying is recorded in Matthew 13:10–17, Mark 4:10–12, and Luke 8:9–10.

Jesus Teaches the People by the Sea (James Tissot, c. 1886–96)

Views on Jesus's Saying about Parables

Why, you may wonder, would Jesus ever want to deliberately hide truth from the thousands of people who gathered to hear him? After all, the common view is that Christ used parables to make it *easier* to understand him—not harder. Today, there are three main opinions about Matthew 13:11.

1. Jesus never made this statement.

Some theologians believe the Gospel writers invented this saying of Jesus because they simply couldn't understand his teaching, or they were manufacturing a reason to explain why the Jewish religious leaders refused to believe in Jesus. Others suggest the writers made an error in grammar usage or in understanding their own Aramaic language. For these theologians, to believe otherwise seems absurd because they doubt Jesus would deliberately hide truth from anybody.

2. Jesus was describing the inevitable.

This is probably the most popular view among evangelical theologians. It says that Jesus was speaking about what God already knew would happen. Since the religious leaders had not believed in Jesus, he knew it would be impossible for them to understand his teachings. Along these lines, theologian Larry Richards suggests that the religious leaders and crowds of that time had already heard the plain truth about Jesus and refused to believe, so Christ was now leaving them to their unbelief. Richards says, "Jesus began to speak in parables only when it was too late for that first-century generation to turn and find forgiveness."[5]

3. Jesus's statement means exactly what it says.

This is a common perspective among more conservative theologians, both evangelical and mainstream. In this view, some people are enabled by God to receive "the secrets of the Kingdom." Others, by God's sovereign choice, are not. In support of this, they point to similar statements by Jesus in other contexts—for instance,

Matthew 11:25–26; Luke 10:21–22; 19:41–42; and John 12:39–40. Jesus spoke in parables, Millard Erickson explains, because his disciples "were not as spiritually incapacitated as were the other hearers.... It was a special action of God that made the difference between the disciples and the spiritually blind and deaf."[6]

All these viewpoints have been strongly defended in academic settings. Yet as New Testament scholar Timothy Paul Jones points out, "There is a paradox here that we can't solve: God makes people able to see the beauties of Jesus, and yet there is an authentic human response. Both are wholly true, and neither can be ignored."[7]

Perhaps we can never fully understand the reasoning Jesus gave for teaching in parables—something that is God's privilege anyway. However, we can focus on the fact that, thanks to the Gospel writers and the testimony of Scripture as a whole, we've been counted among God's insiders to his "secrets of the Kingdom." For whatever reason, we've been freely given that which the multitudes in Jesus's time were not: unobstructed access and insight into the many parables of Christ.

There is a paradox here that we can't solve: God makes people able to see the beauties of Jesus, and yet there is an authentic human response. Both are wholly true, and neither can be ignored.

—Timothy Paul Jones

It can be unsettling to read the hard sayings of Jesus, like this one in Matthew 13:10–17. Our first instinct is often to reject them, rationalize them, ignore them, or explain them away. It's also sometimes difficult to determine when Christ's statements are universal in nature (meaning they apply to everyone for all time) and when they were intended only for the time and place in which he spoke them. How do we handle this confusion?

As people of faith, we must be willing at times to lay aside our need to fully understand everything and accept what the Spirit of God may or may not choose to reveal to us in our daily lives. This is particularly true when we try to uncover why Jesus taught in parables.

We can see and understand (and argue about) abstract theologies only to a point, since we are capable only of seeing "through a glass darkly" (1 Cor. 13:12 KJV). But we don't always have to understand the "why" behind God's actions; we can choose instead to focus on our response to his actions. The fact is, Jesus taught in parables, and by God's grace we have the insider's view into these powerful stories. What a privilege!

Life Application Questions

1. Although Jesus's disciples were "permitted to understand the secrets of the Kingdom of Heaven" (Matt. 13:11), they often didn't understand what Jesus was doing or saying. In what ways can you relate?

2. Since you have access to the writings of Jesus's disciples (the New Testament), you are one who is "permitted to understand" the meaning of Jesus's parables. What does that mean to you?

3. What is your opinion of the idea that we don't always have to understand the "why" behind God's actions?

4. Looking at Matthew 13:16, what blessings in your life can you attribute to having eyes that "see" and ears that "hear"?

5. Tomorrow, amid the busyness of your day, what key points do you hope to remember from today's session on Matthew 13:10–17?

Living Outside the Book

Now it's time to take your study outside of this book and into your daily life. Try this: *On one of your social media platforms, post the passage for Matthew 13:10–17 and ask, "What are your thoughts on this?"*

Observe who answers and how they respond. Don't try to argue a point of view or "correct" what you might see as someone's bad theology. And don't post your own thoughts unless someone specifically asks for them. Simply solicit opinions and be sure to graciously thank everyone for sharing their thoughts.

Afterward, take the responses to Jesus in prayer, asking him to show you what can be learned from the insights and opinions of your social media connections.

Notes

2 THE VINEYARD WORKERS

Parables about God's Nature

The Vineyard Workers

Here is an interesting question to think about: *Does God owe us anything?* The way we answer is important because it influences the way we view God and his activity in our lives. Considering that he created us, it's true that what God wants to do with us and for us is his choice (see Rom. 9:21). At the same time, however, God promises to give us "everything we need for living a godly life" (2 Peter 1:3).

Simon Peter said to Jesus in Matthew 19:27, "We've given up everything to follow you. What will we get?" This question is the spark that prompted Jesus to teach the Parable of the Vineyard Workers. Jesus reassured Peter there would be many rewards waiting for them in his kingdom, but he also included a caveat: "Many who are the greatest now will be least important then, and those who seem least important now will be the greatest then" (Matt. 19:30).

Then, only a single breath later, Jesus launched into the Parable of the Vineyard Workers to drive home his point, repeating his caveat at the end by saying, "So those who are last now will be first then, and those who are first will be last" (Matt. 20:16). What did Jesus mean by all of this, and what does the answer to this question reveal about God's nature? Let's explore this parable now to see what we can discover.

Key Bible Passage

For this session, read Matthew 20:1–16.

Optional Reading

Explore Matthew 19:23–30, which reveals the conversation that led up to Jesus telling the Parable of the Vineyard Workers, and read Isaiah 5:1–7, which is an Old Testament prophetic parable describing the nation of Israel as God's vineyard.

Other parables about God's nature:

- The Creditor and the Two Debtors (Luke 7:41–43)
- A Friend in Need (Luke 11:5–13)
- The Barren Fig Tree (Luke 13:6–9)
- The Persistent Widow (Luke 18:1–8)

Should you be jealous because I am kind to others?

MATTHEW 20:15

Know It

1. Who are the main characters in this parable, and what are their roles?

2. How much does the foreman pay each worker at the end of the day, and in what order does he pay them? Describe the workers' reaction.

3. How would you summarize the landowner's response to the workers at the end of the parable?

Context of the Parable of the Vineyard Workers

1

Jesus responded to the rich man's question about how to obtain eternal life (Matt. 19:16–22).

2

Jesus used this encounter as a teaching opportunity for the disciples (Matt. 19:23–30).

3

Jesus illustrated his teaching by telling the Parable of the Vineyard Workers (Matt. 20:1–16).

4

Jesus concluded with his summary point: "Those who are last now will be first then, and those who are first will be last" (Matt. 20:16).

Events Leading Up to the Parable

Courtesy of the arbitrary chapter break in our Bibles, the Parable of the Vineyard Workers seems to be a stand-alone moment in Matthew 20. However, it is actually a continuation of a conversation that began in Matthew 19:16, when a rich man asked Jesus what good deed he could do to earn a place in God's eternal kingdom. Jesus responded by telling the man to obey God's commandments and, if he wanted to be perfect, to sell everything he owned, give his profits to the poor, and become one of his followers. The rich man went away sad, realizing he could never earn God's gift because he didn't want to let go of his many possessions.

The Rich Young Ruler
(Harold Copping, c. 1920s)

Then Jesus told his disciples, "I tell you the truth, it is very hard for a rich person to enter the Kingdom of Heaven" (Matt. 19:23). The disciples were concerned by his statement and asked Jesus how *anyone* could be saved in light of these strict conditions. Jesus answered, "Humanly speaking, it is impossible. But with God everything is possible" (Matt. 19:26). Yet Peter, apparently, was still holding on to the idea that his good works held more value than God's free gift of salvation. He said to Jesus, "We've given up everything to follow you. What will we [the twelve disciples] get?" (Matt. 19:27).

Getting to the Point

It is only in this context from Matthew 19 that we can begin to understand the meaning of the Parable of the Vineyard Workers in Matthew 20. What was Jesus's main point in telling this parable as part of his answer to Peter? It probably wasn't about the economics of workers and their wages, since the conversation leading up to this parable is all about the kingdom of heaven, salvation, and other spiritual matters. Was it mainly a moral lesson about equality? That's a good sentiment, but in the parable, the landowner actually treats his workers quite differently. More likely, the Parable of the Vineyard Workers appears to be about the nature of God himself (represented by the landowner), as summed up in his self-description: "I am kind" (Matt. 20:15)—or as the New International Version (NIV) phrases it, "I am generous."

The landowner demonstrates generosity by providing for others so they can benefit from his wealth; God, by comparison, shows generosity by providing what is humanly impossible to gain: eternal life in his kingdom. What's so unique is that God's generosity is not reserved for those who work hardest to earn it. Rather, his grace is freely given to *anyone* who answers his call—even those who respond at the very end of the day, so to speak. In this kind of generosity, then, "those who are last now will be first then, and those who are first will be last" (Matt. 20:16).

A vineyard in central Israel

Meaning of "First" and "Last"

What specifically are we to make of the symbolism represented by the "first" and "last" workers in this parable? Neither Jesus nor his original twelve disciples ever gave a clear definition of whom these workers represent; it was apparently obvious to them which people he was talking about. We're not so fortunate in that regard, and as a result, numerous theories have been presented. The traditional view is that

- the "first" workers represent God's chosen people (Israel) who lived before the time of Jesus—specifically, those who trusted in God's promise to send a Messiah to atone for Israel's sin; and
- the "last" workers represent God's chosen people—"the commonwealth of Israel" (Eph. 2:12 ESV), comprised of Jews and gentiles (non-Jews) who live after Jesus and trust him to forgive their sins.

Still, there are other possibilities, so let's summarize them here:

1. The church father Origen (who lived about two hundred years after Christ) suggested that the first workers represent Adam at the time of creation. After that, the groups of workers symbolized, in succession, Noah, Abraham, Moses, and Jesus and the gentiles.
2. Others see the first workers as the historically self-righteous Pharisees, and the last workers as "tax collectors and other sinners" (Mark 2:16) who were flocking to Jesus during his earthly ministry.

3. One final possibility, given Simon Peter's question in Matthew 19:27 ("What will we get?"), is that the first workers could represent Jesus's original disciples. The last workers are "tax collectors and other sinners" and gentile believers who would become Jesus's followers throughout the rest of history.

Regardless of whom the workers symbolize in this parable, one core fact is true: *God is generous toward all*. That's simply his nature. When we see him blessing others in ways that appear unfair in comparison to the way he blesses each of us, our response need not be jealousy or anger. Instead, we can rejoice in the knowledge that we serve a proactively generous Savior, who extends his grace to us both now and throughout eternity.

Parable of the Vineyard Workers: Key Symbols

SYMBOL	WHAT IS REPRESENTED
Landowner	God the Father, who created the world and made a covenant with Abraham, Isaac, and Jacob (renamed Israel)
Vineyard	The nation of Israel, God's chosen people, who today are known as Jews, regardless of their citizenship
First Workers	God's chosen people (Israel) who lived before Christ and trusted in God's promise to send a Messiah to atone for Israel's sin
Last Workers	The commonwealth of Israel—Jews and gentiles after Christ who are saved from sin by trusting in Jesus's atoning death and resurrection
Foreman	Angels who enact God's justice in the end times

More than a few takeaways from this parable still resonate today. The primary message is that *God is generous*—and yet in being generous, he doesn't treat everyone the same. The workers are all paid the same (equally)—but treated very differently. That's why some of the workers are so upset: They feel they've been treated unfairly in comparison to the others. The first workers labored an entire day to receive their reward; others labored as little as one hour for the same reward. Interestingly, the landowner made sure the first workers saw that inequity happen. He instructed the foreman to pay the last workers first, in full view of the others, so he never intended to hide his "unfair" generosity from others. Have you ever seen someone receive a blessing from God you thought they didn't deserve—or that made you believe you deserved more? If this hasn't happened to you yet, keep your eyes open, because it won't be long!

Perhaps it helps to think of it in terms of a mother who loves all her children equally, but her love is fine-tuned to express itself in ways that consider each child's needs, interests, and capabilities. She might ask her oldest child to wash all the dishes, while her middle child is assigned to clear the table, and the youngest must eat all her vegetables before she is excused from dinner. Equal love requires unique expression (treatment) that is suited to the one who is loved. And so it is with God, as this parable teaches us. He is generous toward all, and in his perfect love he treats each of us according to our distinct calling, purpose, personality, and circumstances, as he sees fit.

Life Application Questions

1. The landowner went out searching for workers instead of waiting for laborers to come to him asking for work. Why do you think Jesus included that specific story detail?

2. "The normal daily wage" paid by the landowner was one Roman denarius—about enough to buy grain for two days' worth of bread (Matt. 20:2). Why do you suppose God's provision is often not intended as a long-term gain?

3. Which view classifying the identity of the "first" and "last" workers seems most accurate to you, and why?

4. How have you personally benefited from God's generous nature? If you have ever struggled with resenting his generosity toward others, describe how your perspective may have changed through this study.

5. What difference will your study of this parable make in your life tomorrow? Be specific.

Living Outside the Book

Now it's time to take your study outside of this book and into your daily life. Try this: *Find one way to imitate God this week by being generous.* For instance, you might:

- Buy coffee for the person behind you in line at the café.
- Donate something you'd actually like to keep, but which you know will make another person happy.
- Volunteer somewhere that is outside your normal routine—check your city's official website for community volunteer opportunities.
- Grab a trash bag and some gloves and spend a half hour picking up litter in your neighborhood or at the local park.
- Or anything else you might dream up between now and next week!

Notes

Parables about Judgment

The Sheep and the Goats

Jesus's Parable of the Sheep and the Goats presents two challenges. First, there's an open question as to whether it's a parable at all. Although it does contain symbolic imagery and is often titled as a parable in headings used by various Bible translations, some see this passage as a more literal description of divine realities to come at the end of time. As you read Matthew 25:31–46 for this study, think about whether you would categorize this as a parable, a prophetic picture of a future event, or both.

Second, some may have a difficult time understanding how actions taken by the "sheep"—and not taken by the "goats"—are the determining factor for divine judgment. After all, doesn't the Bible clearly indicate that salvation is merited by faith alone (Luke 7:48–50; John 3:16; Rom. 3:28; 4:5; Gal. 2:16)? How is it, then, that this parable seems to indicate the "sheep" inherit God's kingdom and eternal life based on deeds they performed? Similarly, if good deeds are not a prerequisite for salvation, why is a significant portion of humanity thrown "into the eternal fire prepared for the devil and his demons" (Matt. 25:41) simply because they failed to act mercifully toward others—especially in light of the fact they didn't commit any outright evil or violence? Let's take some time to find out.

Read It

Key Bible Passage

For this session, read Matthew 25:31–46.

Optional Reading

Explore other prophecies of judgment in Psalm 96:11–13, Daniel 7:9–10, and Ezekiel 34:17–22, as well as God's perspective on those who are poor and in need in Deuteronomy 15:7–11, Proverbs 14:31, and Proverbs 19:17.

Other parables about judgment:

- The Wheat and Weeds (Matt. 13:24–30, 36–43)
- The Evil Farmers (Matt. 21:33–46; Mark 12:1–12; Luke 20:9–19)
- The Great Feast (Matt. 22:1–14; Luke 14:15–24)
- The Faithful and Unfaithful Servants (Matt. 24:45–51; Luke 12:42–48)
- The Rich Man and Lazarus (Luke 16:19–31)

> I was hungry, and you fed me. I was thirsty, and you gave me a drink. I was a stranger, and you invited me into your home.
>
> MATTHEW 25:35

Know It

1. What six actions are taken by the "sheep" and neglected by the "goats"?

1. ____

2. ____

3. ____

4. ____

5. ____

6. ____

2. According to Jesus, who did the "sheep" and the "goats" ultimately help or harm, and what is the eternal fate of each group?

3. The "sheep" appear to have no idea that by showing kindness, they were serving Jesus. What do you suppose was their motivation if it wasn't a heavenly reward?

The Importance of Compassion

What's most surprising about Jesus's Parable of the Sheep and the Goats is not that there is a coming judgment where some will be rewarded and others condemned. Rather, what stands out is that none of the people described here—represented by the sheep and the goats—had a clue that the consideration they gave to others reflected the level of consideration they had for God himself.

But was that ignorance justified? After all, they would have been familiar with the Jewish Scriptures (the Christian Old Testament), which clearly teach that people are crafted by God's hand in his own image: "God created human beings in his own image. In the image of God he created them" (Gen. 1:27). In one sense, then, the "sheep" and the "goats" would have understood that how they treated people boiled down to how they treated God. Both groups would have also been familiar with commands in the Jewish Scriptures to treat the poor with love, compassion, and justice. Certainly their economic and social status did not negate that they, too, are precious to God and created in his image.

When we look at the six issues Jesus raised in this parable—hunger, thirst, hospitality to strangers, lack of clothing, sickness, and imprisonment—it seems clear that he deliberately chose these specific examples of compassion to demonstrate the principle of "faith expressing itself in love" (Gal. 5:6). Each situation was a common experience for those who were poor and oppressed throughout Israel's history, but Israel had mostly ignored the Scriptures about caring for these people. About seven hundred years before Jesus was born, the Lord spoke through the prophet Isaiah to rebuke Israel for their hypocritical behavior:

> Tell my people Israel of their sins! Yet they act so pious! … "We have fasted before you!" they say. "Why aren't you impressed?" … "I will tell you why!" I respond. "It's because you are fasting to please yourselves.... No, this is the kind of fasting I want: *Free those who are wrongly imprisoned*; lighten the burden of those who work for you. *Let the oppressed go free*, and *remove the chains that bind people. Share your food with the hungry*, and *give shelter to the homeless. Give clothes to those who need them*, and do not hide from relatives who need your help. *Then your salvation will come* like the dawn, and your wounds will quickly heal.
>
> **ISAIAH 58:1–8**

When Jesus indicated in the Parable of the Sheep and the Goats that showing compassion was a characteristic of those who would inherit eternal salvation, he was mostly echoing the voice of the Old Testament Scriptures that had been preserved for centuries. The six characteristics he gave should not have surprised his disciples or any others who may have heard this parable.

Visiting the Prisoners

"I was in prison, and you visited me," Jesus proclaimed in verse 36 of this parable. Back in those days, what was so important about stopping by a prison to say hi to your favorite prisoner? The reality is that Jesus was most likely speaking about "debtor's prison," not our current perception of criminal incarceration. Here is what we know about debtor's prison:

- In first-century Israel, it was common practice that those who were too poor to repay a debt were imprisoned until the debt was paid in full (see Matt. 5:25–26 and Luke 12:58–59). Of course, repayment was impossible unless someone on the outside intervened.
- Debtor's prison was not known for feeding its prisoners well. In fact, family members and friends were often responsible for providing enough food for the debtor. Otherwise, he or she would likely die of malnutrition.
- It was common for guards to demand bribes from visitors before allowing them access to a prisoner. Thus, in addition to providing food and helping to pay off the debt, family members would also have to pay off a guard or two. This would have been especially burdensome for visitors who were living in near poverty, as many were.

As you can see, Jesus made a big deal about visiting debtor's prison because *it was a big deal*. It was costly, required both time and physical sacrifice, and was truly an act of love toward someone who was completely helpless. We have it easy by comparison.

The High Cost of Debtor's Prison

The debtor's family members and friends helped repay the debt as they were able.

Family and friends provided the debtor with life-sustaining food.

Family and friends often had to bribe the prison guards.

The Role of Good Works

This end-times scene with the sheep and the goats does raise one surprising question for us today: *Was Jesus saying that good works are the requirement for receiving eternal life in heaven?* At first blush this might seem a reasonable assumption, but it ignores a few important points:

1. It appears the sheep did not consciously do good works for the result of an eternal reward. As one theologian put it, "That both the sheep and the goats are surprised at their 'qualifications' indicates that neither was working for salvation."[8]
2. The New Testament as a whole—including Jesus's own words—indicates that good works are the *result* of his grace, not the *cause* of it (see John 6:44; 15:1–8; Rom. 9:16; Eph. 2:8–10).

The best answer to this question comes from James, the half-brother of Jesus. He explains that faith that is living and active will *naturally express itself* in loving acts—and those acts, then, are visible proof that God's Spirit has changed the invisible heart inside of a person (see James 2:14–26). Thus, the good works of compassion that were undertaken by the sheep are a reflection of the saving faith they already possessed—not a means of earning it. Likewise, the lack of compassion demonstrated by the goats is an indicator that they lacked saving faith, resulting in "eternal punishment" (Matt. 25:46).

Faith Equals Action

Suppose you see a brother or sister who has no food or clothing, and you say, "Good-bye and have a good day; stay warm and eat well"—but then you don't give that person any food or clothing. What good does that do? So you see, faith by itself isn't enough. Unless it produces good deeds, it is dead and useless.

—James 2:15–17

Live It

Intelligent minds throughout history have spent a lot of time and energy dissecting the Parable of the Sheep and the Goats. They dig into cultural issues, end-times interpretations, phrasing used in the original Greek manuscripts, and much more. Still, what most scholars and thinkers miss about the parable is this: *What you do with your life matters.*

When you love others because Christ first loved you (1 John 4:19), the simple daily services you perform in his name have a never-ending impact. Taking a sick friend to the doctor or dropping off items at a thrift store or food bank may seem mundane, but to Jesus, they are holy, spectacular actions that showcase your faith expressing itself through love. Such faith and actions will reap *eternal* rewards at the final judgment. There is nothing mundane about that!

Life Application Questions

1. In your opinion, is Matthew 25:31–46 a parable, a prophecy of events to come, or both? Does believing one way or the other affect how you respond to its message?

2. If "eternal fire" is being "prepared for the devil and his demons" (Matt. 25:41), why do you think billions of humanity's "goats" will be included in this horrible destiny?

3. Considering you have limited time and resources to work with, what are some ways you can demonstrate compassion in the ways that Jesus illustrates in this parable? Brainstorm three ideas.

1. ____

2. ____

3. ____

4. Does the "eternal punishment" (Matt. 25:46) that Jesus spoke of prompt you to pray in a particular way? Write out a specific prayer and wait for Jesus's response as you go about your daily tasks.

5. What is the most important insight from your study of this parable that you want to carry with you each day this week?

Living Outside the Book

Now it's time to take your study outside of this book and into your real life. *Do one of the following acts of mercy:*

Feed the hungry. Contact a local food bank and ask how you can volunteer. If there are no such organizations in your area, contact the Salvation Army and ask how you can donate to their food pantries ministry. Learn more at salvationarmyusa.org/usn/cure-hunger.

Provide water for the thirsty. Donate time or resources to The Water Project, an organization that builds wells to provide clean, sanitary water to people living in sub-Saharan Africa. Learn more at thewaterproject.org/clean-water-wells-in-africa.

Practice hospitality. Explore becoming a host family for a foreign exchange student. When you do this, you are literally inviting a stranger into your home. Find more information about this option at the Ayusa International website: ayusa.org.

Give clothing to those in need. You can do this through the ministry of a local church or by donating to thrift stores like Goodwill (goodwill.org), Dress for Success (dressforsuccess.org), and The Arc Store (arcthrift.com).

Care for the sick. Contact your nearest cancer center and ask, "How can I be helpful?" You'll be surprised at how many volunteer opportunities are available. You can also check out Phil's Friends (philsfriends.org) or the American Cancer Society's volunteer page (cancer.org/involved/volunteer.html).

Visit the prisoners. Chances are very good that a church in your community—maybe even yours—has a prison ministry. See if you can tag along on one of their visits, just to observe. Who knows—you may like it and want to make a return visit! If there isn't a prison ministry near you, consider helping out the national ministry of Prison Fellowship (prisonfellowship.org).

Notes

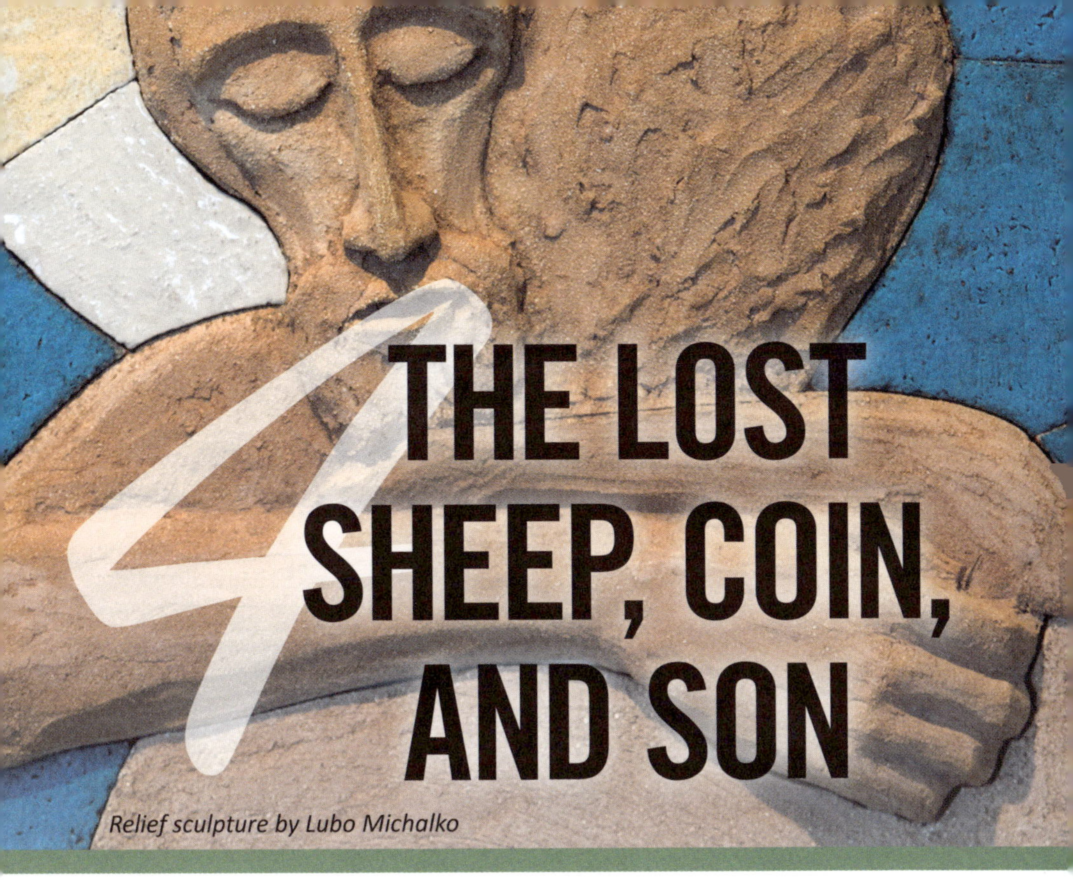

4 THE LOST SHEEP, COIN, AND SON

Relief sculpture by Lubo Michalko

Parables about Redemption

The Lost Sheep, Coin, and Son

If Jesus had been telling his parables about "lost" things in this day and age, it's not a stretch to imagine that he might have included one called "The Parable of the Lost Cell Phone." Perhaps you could be the main character in such a parable: Things are going along just fine and then—bam! You realize you have no idea where you left your mobile phone.

Whatever you were doing becomes secondary to *finding that blasted little device*. If you're lucky, there is someone nearby who can call your cell; then you can (hopefully) hear it ringing and track it down that way. If you're not so lucky, you'll spend half a day searching every pocket in your clothing and every nook, cranny, and drawer in your house ... until you finally give up, slump onto your couch, and discover your phone between the cushions. And then there's rejoicing in the presence of the angels, right? (Or at least you're pretty happy about it!)

Similarly, the message of Luke 15 is that God cares deeply about lost things—particularly, about people who've wandered from his loving care. In fact, God treasures us so much that Jesus told not one, not two, but three parables in a row to emphasize that truth.

Read It

Key Bible Passage

For this session, read Luke 15.

Optional Reading

Take a look at these Scriptures from the Old Testament book of Hosea: 1:1–2:1; 3:1–5; 14:1–7. They highlight what is known as an "acted parable"—a real-life situation that communicates a message from God. In the story of Hosea's wife, Gomer, and her symbolic representation of the idolatrous nation of Israel, we see again God's persistent desire for redemption, "to seek and save those who are lost" (Luke 19:10).

Rejoice with me, because I have found my lost sheep.

LUKE 15:6

Know It

1. What reason does Luke give for why Jesus told the parables in chapter 15?

2. When you read these three parables, what common elements do you see?

3. What words would you use to describe the shepherd, the woman, and the father in these parables? Which words stand out to you, and why?

Luke 15 is a unique collection of Jesus's parables—three stories making the same point, all told in response to criticism from religious leaders about his comfortable association with ungodly folk. The entire chapter is steeped in cultural influence, so let's explore some of the backgrounds associated with each major passage.

Luke 15:1–2: Introduction

Jesus made no secret of welcoming "notorious sinners" who were drawn to him and his message of repentance. When the Roman Empire ruled Israel, the religious leaders and much of the Jewish population considered tax collectors to be the most notorious of sinners. Why? Because they worked for the oppressive Roman government, used their position as an opportunity to steal from the common people, and lived lavish, ungodly lifestyles. Most tax collectors would have been guilty of violating several of God's Ten Commandments (Exodus 20:2–17). The fact that Jesus spent time with any kind of sinner disgusted the Pharisees and other religious teachers who were watching him. They especially complained that Jesus ate with such people. But why would they even care about that?

Zacchaeus in the Sycamore Awaiting the Passage of Jesus (James Tissot, c. 1886–96)

During the time of Jesus, voluntarily eating a meal with someone had great significance—it communicated that the person was socially acceptable and worthy of spending time with. At the same time, tax collectors were particularly despised because they were known for their corruption and for actively supporting the occupying Roman authorities. They were universally condemned among the Jews as the most notorious of sinners—even Jesus said as much (see Matt. 5:46; 21:31). The Gospels mention tax collectors nearly two dozen times, and every instance is insulting to some degree. In addition to being guilty of blatant sin in general, tax collectors were linked with specific sins such as gluttony, drunkenness, a pagan lifestyle, and prostitution (see Matt. 11:19; 18:17; 21:31–32).

The Pharisees' legalistic application of the law of Moses declared that even associating with known sinners like tax collectors was something that made them ritually impure, meaning they were unfit for worship at the temple—and going so far as to *eat* with a sinner? Well, that was just a gross disregard for everything they found to be right and holy. Rabbinic advice written down later summed it up this way: "Let not a man associate with the wicked, even to bring him near to the law."[9]

Jesus Visits Zacchaeus

This ancient sycamore tree in Jericho is likely similar to the one the tax collector Zacchaeus climbed as he waited for Jesus to pass:

"Jesus entered Jericho and made his way through the town.... He looked up at Zacchaeus and called him by name. 'Zacchaeus!' he said, 'Quick, come down! I must be a guest in your home today'" (Luke 19:1-5).

Tax Collectors and the Ten Commandments

SCRIPTURE	COMMAND	VIOLATION
Exodus 20:3	1. "You must not have any other god but me."	Tax collectors chose the pursuit of riches over the pursuit of God and his instructions for life.
Exodus 20:4	2. "You must not make for yourself an idol of any kind or an image of anything in the heavens or on the earth or in the sea."	Tax collectors made spiritual idols out of the affluence and influence that money brings.
Exodus 20:14	7. "You must not commit adultery."	Casual sex would have likely been an aspect of a tax collector's lifestyle, as suggested by Jesus's reference to "tax collectors and prostitutes" (Matt. 21:31).
Exodus 20:15	8. "You must not steal."	Tax collectors were known for overcharging and pocketing the difference.
Exodus 20:16	9. "You must not testify falsely against your neighbor."	In order to overcharge, tax collectors would lie about what was actually due.
Exodus 20:17	10. "You must not covet ... anything ... that belongs to your neighbor."	The tax collector's career was built on illegally acquiring a neighbor's money and possessions.

Luke 15:3–7: Parable of the Lost Sheep

The Parable of the Lost Sheep is one of the most famous of Jesus's stories, depicting a good shepherd so passionate that he leaves the main flock to seek out one lost lamb (it's also told in Matt. 18:12–14). In that time and culture, sheep and shepherds were commonplace and necessary for everyday survival and temple sacrifices. Historians estimate that an average shepherd's flock consisted of about one hundred sheep. The shepherd's sole job was to protect and care for all the sheep in the herd. That a shepherd might be willing to risk the safety of ninety-nine sheep—his entire livelihood—just to search out one lost lamb would have been surprising to Jesus's hearers. Even today, theologians struggle with how to explain that circumstance.

The Good Shepherd
(James Tissot, c. 1886–94)

For instance, Archbishop Dmitri Royster of the Orthodox Church in America asked, "Does that mean that he [the shepherd] is willing to risk losing many more for the sake of one? Or are they perfectly safe and not apt to become lost because they are in a familiar grazing place?"[10] Other scholars such as Craig Keener speculate that "because shepherds often traveled together, this shepherd could probably leave his flock with his companions without endangering the flock."[11] One other opinion is that the shepherd leaving the ninety-nine sheep "in the wilderness" (15:4) was intended to simply mean that "the shepherd delayed taking the rest [of the flock] home until he found the lost sheep."[12] Regardless, Jesus was unconcerned with providing an explanation about the safety of the ninety-nine who stayed with the flock. His emphasis was on the shepherd's concern for each individual sheep.

Luke 15:8–10: Parable of the Lost Coin

The fact that Jesus included such descriptive details in the Parable of the Lost Coin seems to indicate that he was very familiar with the situation he presented—and he expected his hearers to be likewise familiar. We know from the original Greek text that the word translated "coin" refers to a silver drachma—a common Greek coin that was roughly equivalent to one day's wage. So while it certainly had value, it wasn't exactly a pile of riches. Bible historian John Beck observes, "The woman enacts an aggressive search for the lost coin that seems incompatible with the coin's value. And when she finds it, she calls her friends and neighbors together for a celebration that seems a bit over the top for the coin's value."[13]

Some theologians believe the ten silver coins were part of the woman's dowry. Meager though it was, that dowry would have carried special significance to her and was probably worn as part of a decorative necklace or headdress. To lose one coin from that setting would have been concerning, which could also explain why the woman would spend so much time and energy to retrieve and celebrate it. As for sweeping the house, it seems that ancient homes of poor folk like this woman in Israel used rough stones for flooring. There were so many cracks and crevices that coins and pottery shards found in them today are used by archaeologists to actually determine how old a home might be.

Ancient drachma

Luke 15:11–32: Parable of the Lost Son

The Return of the Prodigal Son
(Rembrandt, c. 1667–70)

Mining the richness of the Parable of the Lost Son (or Prodigal Son) could fill the pages of many books. Just like today, an inheritance in those times did not pass from a parent to a child until after the parent died. To Jesus's hearers, demanding a future inheritance from your *living* dad was a grave insult that pretty much communicated the idea, "I wish you were dead already!"

We know the younger son as a "prodigal" because, after receiving a fortune, he simply wasted it all. In fact, the term *prodigal* literally means "wasteful." After throwing away his inheritance on "wild living" (v. 13), the younger son was reduced to feeding pigs for a foreign swine herder. Nineteenth-century pastor and theologian Albert Barnes explained why that would sound horrific to a first-century Jew: "It was forbidden for the Jews to eat swine, and of course it was unlawful to keep them. To be compelled, therefore, to engage in such an employment was the deepest conceivable degradation.... Nothing could more strikingly show the evil of his condition."[14]

At that point, most of Jesus's Jewish listeners probably expected him to end the story there. After all, the son got what he deserved for his sinful, disrespectful actions. Imagine their surprise when the son not only returned home but was also welcomed with joy by his father running to meet him. "Even today," says New Testament scholar Mark Strauss, "a distinguished Middle Eastern patriarch in robes does not run, but always walks in a slow and dignified manner. Running was viewed as humiliating and degrading."[15]

To solidify his standing as a son, the father gave him a fine robe, a ring, and sandals. The robe could have been one reserved for honored guests, but most likely it was one of the father's own robes, which would have been the nicest in the house. The ring was likely a family signet ring—not just a finger decoration, but one used as an official seal to authorize agreements for the family. Because servants and slaves didn't typically wear shoes, providing the son with sandals indicated he was not to be treated as anything less than a son in the household.

Signet ring from the Byzantine period

And that "fattened calf" (v. 30) for the party? Bible historians tell us it would have been enough to feed an entire village, so it's likely that the whole town was invited to celebrate the lost son's return to his joyous father.

Live It

After reading the parables in Luke 15, it's easy to think, *Wow, God loves me so much he'll go to great lengths just to bring me back to him!* Such a sentiment is true and good and delivers genuine hope. What we often skim over, however, is what prompted Jesus to tell these stories in the first place: the fact that Jesus loves "awful" people. He spent time with them and even ate meals with them, to the extent that it deeply angered the religious "good" people who observed it.

This is great news if you're one of the "awful" people, but chances are you picked up this study because you're one of the "good" ones. You probably read your Bible, go to church, and donate money or time to good causes. Maybe you even avoid spending too much time with, or even accepting, the "awful" people God has allowed in your life.

Yet the message of Jesus's parables in Luke 15 is pretty straightforward. The way we adopt his values in that message, the way we live out his redeeming heart in our daily experience ... well, that's not so easy, is it? How do we love, accept, and associate with "awful" people whom God loves, without endorsing or enabling sinful behavior? None of us knows the full answer to that question, but Jesus certainly does. We can go to him in full confidence, asking him to help us better love those he loves—even when they're people we prefer to dislike or ignore.

Life Application Questions

1. Religious leaders of Jesus's day were offended that he welcomed "tax collectors and other notorious sinners" (Luke 15:1). What kind of "sinners" are offensive to people in your church today? And to you personally?

2. The Parable of the Lost Sheep and the Parable of the Lost Coin describe a main character (who represents God) losing something moderately valuable, then risking or spending more than its perceived worth to regain it. What do you make of that oddity?

3. How does the almighty, omniscient, ever-present, eternal God *lose* anyone?

4. When were you "lost"? How did God "find" you?

5. God and his angels rejoice greatly at the fact that you've been found. How can you join that celebration?

Living Outside the Book

Now it's time to take your study outside of this book and into your real life. Try this: *Write a short story that demonstrates the same message of Luke 15, but use new characters and settings.*

Let yourself be creative with the storyline. For instance, how about a *Star Wars*–style "space opera" of the prodigal son? Or a modern-day sitcom about the woman who lost a coin? Or a sports drama about the Fighting Lambkins and their coach who is trying to keep the team together after a star player decides to quit?

Before you write, answer these questions:

- Who or what is lost, and how did it happen?
- Who goes looking for the lost character or item, and why?
- What challenges stand in the way?
- How is the lost character or item found?

After that, you're ready! Write up your brand-new parable, and when you're finished, share it with your family, friends, coworkers, and others who might enjoy it. Have fun!

Notes

Parables about Right Living

The Good Samaritan

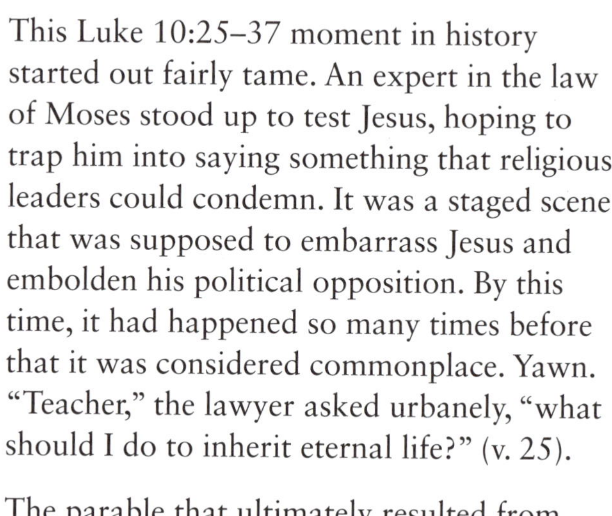

This Luke 10:25–37 moment in history started out fairly tame. An expert in the law of Moses stood up to test Jesus, hoping to trap him into saying something that religious leaders could condemn. It was a staged scene that was supposed to embarrass Jesus and embolden his political opposition. By this time, it had happened so many times before that it was considered commonplace. Yawn. "Teacher," the lawyer asked urbanely, "what should I do to inherit eternal life?" (v. 25).

The parable that ultimately resulted from this question has become the most famous in history: The Good Samaritan. It's a story about two other experts in the law of Moses who are put in their place by a lowly, despised, half-breed, theologically heretical *Samaritan*. Almost as if to rub the lawyer's nose in it, Jesus forced him to declare that the worst person in the story—the Samaritan—is actually the best.

All of this resulted from a simple question the lawyer already knew the answer to. *How did it end up like this?* he must have wondered. Jesus didn't contradict anything he had said during their conversation, so how was anybody going to be upset about that? And why was the story about the Good Samaritan so embarrassing for him and the religious leaders he represented? Let's find out.

Read It

Key Bible Passage

For this session, read Luke 10:25–37.

Optional Reading

Read Luke 11:37–53 to learn what Jesus really thought of the experts of religious law in his time. Matthew 22:34–40 records another time that Jesus was questioned by an expert in the law of Moses. You can also read Deuteronomy 6:1–5 and Leviticus 19:18, which the lawyer partially quoted to Jesus in Luke 10:27, as well as 2 Kings 17, which recounts how Samaritan history began.

Other parables about right living:

- The Lamp (Matt. 5:14–16; Mark 4:21–22; Luke 8:16–17; 11:33–36)
- Building on a Solid Foundation (Matt. 7:24–27; Luke 6:47–49)
- The Two Sons (Matt. 21:28–32)
- The Rich Fool (Luke 12:16–21)
- The Place of Honor (Luke 14:7–11)
- The Shrewd Manager (Luke 16:1–13)
- The Pharisee and Tax Collector (Luke 18:9–14)

A despised Samaritan came along, and when he saw the man, he felt compassion for him.

LUKE 10:33

Know It

1. How does Jesus answer the lawyer's question, "What should I do to inherit eternal life?" (Luke 10:25)? What are some examples for living out Jesus's answer in everyday life?

2. What actions are taken by the priest, the temple assistant, and the Samaritan?

3. List at least three principles of right living that you see acted out in the Parable of the Good Samaritan.

Parable of the Good Samaritan

WORD OR PHRASE	INSIGHT
Luke 10:25: "expert in religious law"	In ancient Israel, the law of Moses addressed all criminal, civil, and religious laws. This "expert," then, had a career of studying and teaching the Torah (the first five books of the Old Testament, which contain the law of Moses), as well as the rabbinical interpretations regarding them.
Luke 10:29: "neighbor"	In strict Jewish understanding, "neighbor" would have applied only to a fellow Israelite. However, some Jewish leaders were arguing for "neighbor" to apply to all humankind—a controversy the religious law expert may have been addressing when he asked, "Who is my neighbor?"
Luke 10:30: "down to Jericho"	The road from Jerusalem to Jericho was a short 20-mile span that dropped more than 2,900 feet, from well above sea level in Jerusalem to about 800 feet below sea level at Jericho.
Luke 10:30: "attacked by bandits"	This stretch of road through the wilderness was notoriously crime infested. For centuries it was actually nicknamed "The Bloody Way." In Jesus's time, King Herod dismissed about 40,000 men who'd been rebuilding the temple, and as the ancient Jewish historian Josephus reported, many of them became robbers and bandits in this area.

WORD OR PHRASE	INSIGHT
Luke 10:33: "a despised Samaritan"	A long history of animosity existed between the Samaritans and Jews.
Luke 10:34: "soothed his wounds"	According to Bible historian Craig Blomberg, "All of the detail surrounding the care given to the wounded man is entirely realistic as the kind of treatment that could and should have been given the man in that day under the circumstances and serves to underline the extent of the Samaritan's love."[16]
Luke 10:34: "took him to an inn"	There are ruins today of an ancient inn built along the road from Jerusalem to Jericho. Some historians think it might have been the inn Jesus used as the model for this parable.
Luke 10:35: "innkeeper"	Innkeepers in Jesus's time were infamous for being dishonest, which is perhaps why the Samaritan gave financial incentive to care for the wounded man.

Beginnings of Samaritan History

Why did Jesus use the word *despised* when describing the Samaritan in this parable (Luke 10:33)? To answer that question, let's look at the history of the Samaritans and their relationship with the Jewish people. Samaritan history began when the Northern Kingdom of Israel and its capital city, Samaria, were conquered by the Assyrian army in 722 BC:

> Samaria fell, and the people of Israel were exiled to Assyria. They were settled in colonies in Halah, along the banks of the Habor River in Gozan, and in the cities of the Medes.
>
> 2 Kings 17:6

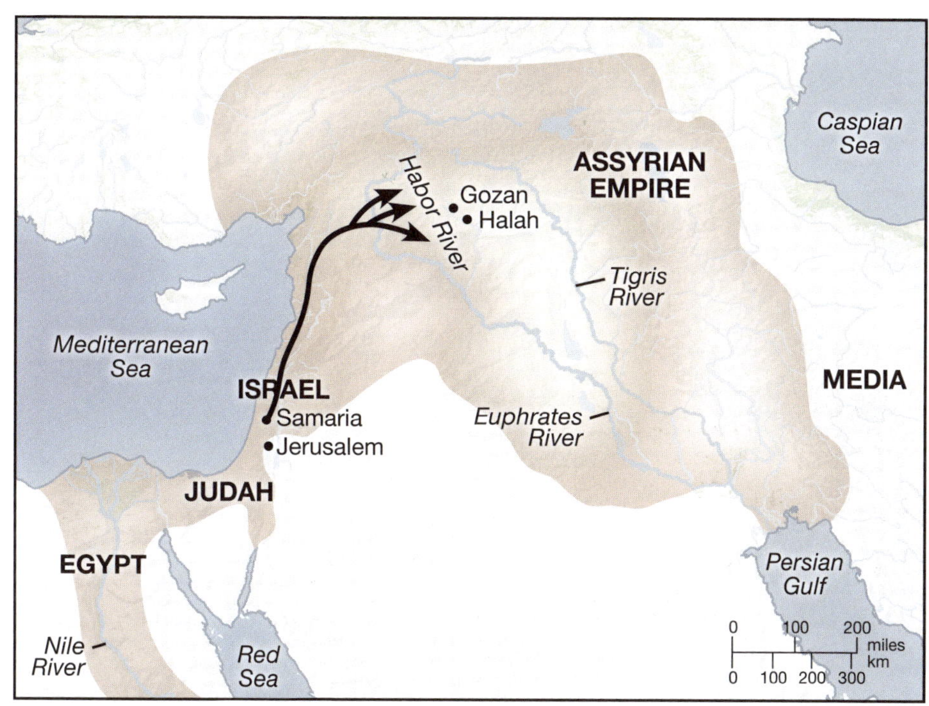

722 BC: Assyria exiles many Israelites and colonizes the Northern Kingdom

The Assyrians also colonized the Northern Kingdom by sending their own people to live there (2 Kings 17:24). Yet, not all the Israelites were exiled to Assyria. Some remained in the land and intermarried with the foreign Assyrians (gentiles) who were brought in. This intermixing, along with the cultural influences of such a varied population, resulted in a new people group who were eventually called Samaritans. Samaritans, however, resisted the idea that they were "half-breeds." They claimed to be pure descendants from the Israelite tribes of Manasseh, Ephraim, and Levi, tracing some of their ancestors back to Israel's first high priest, Aaron.

Samaritans were devoted to the Torah (the first five books of the Old Testament) but dismissed the rest of the Jewish Scriptures (our Old Testament) as invalid. They viewed Moses as the last prophet of God and held tightly to the belief that Mount Gerizim—not Jerusalem—was the only God-approved place for worship. Despite the theological differences between Samaritans and Jews, they held many beliefs in common, including dedication to the one true God,

Yahweh; high respect for Moses; belief in a future judgment of all humans; and hope in the coming of God's Messiah.

Samaritan temple ruins atop Mount Gerizim

Tensions between Jews and Samaritans

In 539 BC, the Persians took control of the land where the Samaritans lived and allowed captive descendants of the Southern Kingdom of Judah to return. The Samaritans and the returning exiles feuded almost immediately. The initial dispute appears to have occurred when Jews returning from exile rebuffed Samaritan offers to help rebuild the temple in Jerusalem (Ezra 4). Later, Nehemiah reported that Sanballat (the Samaritan governor) and others were hotly opposing the rebuilding of the wall around Jerusalem (Nehemiah 2). Sometime during the fifth century BC, the Samaritans built their own temple atop Mount Gerizim, but the Jews considered it sacrilegious to locate God's temple outside of Jerusalem.

About 332 BC, when the Greek Empire began to rule the area, Samaritans antagonized Jews by raiding their land and even taking some Jews as slaves. Additionally, to gain favor with the powerful Greek ruler, the Samaritans denied any association with the Jews and allowed their temple to be dedicated to the Greek god Zeus. This so angered Jews that when they warred for (and won) independence from the Greeks, they also destroyed the city of Samaria and the Samaritan temple, which has never been rebuilt.

In 63 BC, the Roman invasion of the Holy Land freed the Samaritans from Jewish rule. Needless to say, hard feelings between Jews and Samaritans remained. Around AD 8 (while Jesus was a child in Nazareth), a group of Samaritan troublemakers sneaked inside the Jerusalem temple during Passover and scattered the bones of dead people. It was a horrific desecration, because the law of Moses stated that touching the dead made a person unfit to worship at the tabernacle until he or she underwent a seven-day purification process (Num. 19:11–13). This also meant that Jews were prevented from entering the temple area and offering their Passover sacrifices as an act of worship.

Located along the ancient Jerusalem-to-Jericho road, the modern Inn of the Good Samaritan is built over the ruins of an ancient inn. Some historians believe it is the same one Jesus referenced in his parable.

Jesus and the Samaritans

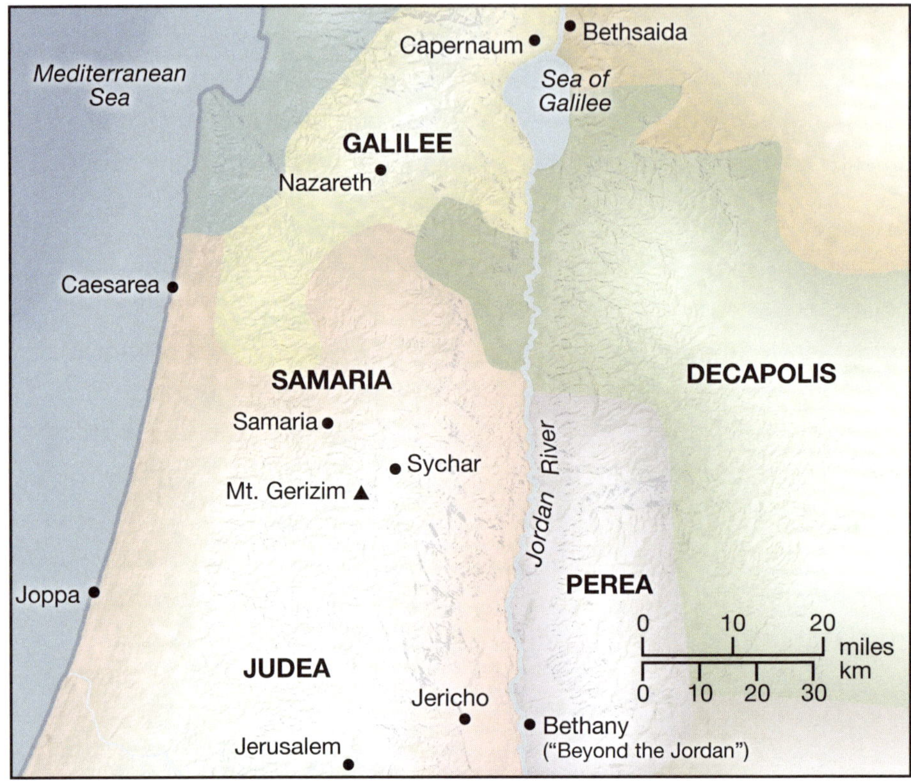

Samaria during the time of Jesus

The Jews and Samaritans continued these kinds of tit-for-tat attacks for most of their history together, to the extent that, by the time of Jesus's ministry, they mostly despised each other. Yet at the same time, they were forced to live near each other, to participate in a joint economy under Roman rule, and to submit to occasional cultural accommodations, such as when both groups were celebrating the same religious festival, or when a Samaritan woman acted as midwife or wet nurse for a Jewish mother.

And what did Jesus think of Samaritans? As one can see from reading the Parable of the Good Samaritan, he was determinedly anti-racist toward them—something that would have been both surprising and offensive to most Jews of that time. Jesus didn't seem to mind, though. Consider: Although the Jewish people tended to divide the world into two groups—Jews and gentiles (non-Jews, including Samaritans)—Jesus repeatedly marked Samaritans as a unique people alongside both Jews and gentiles (Matt. 10:5–6; Acts 1:8). When a Samaritan village rejected Jesus's plans to visit, two of his disciples wanted to call down fire from heaven to kill everyone there. Yet Jesus not only refused to let them commit that kind of genocide but also "rebuked them" in favor of the Samaritan people (Luke 9:51–56).

At one time in his ministry, Jesus entered a village at the border between Galilee (home to Jews) and Samaria (home to Samaritans). Just as he arrived, ten men ravaged by leprosy called out to him, "Jesus, Master, have mercy on us!" Jesus told them to go show themselves to the priests, and as they went on their way, he miraculously healed them. It was a stunning miracle, yet only one of the ten returned to express thanks—and that man was a Samaritan. Jesus endorsed both his faith and his ethnic identity for everyone when he said, "Has no one returned to give glory to God except this foreigner?" (Luke 17:11–19).

Early photo of Jacob's well near Sychar, the traditional site where Jesus spoke to the Samaritan woman

Another time, Jesus was traveling through Samaria with his disciples and stopped to rest by a well in the village of Sychar. While his disciples were in town buying food, he spoke with a Samaritan woman—breaking taboos against the treatment of Samaritans *and* women! Jesus even postponed his journey back to Galilee to stay two full days with the Samaritans. Scripture reports that the woman and many Samaritans in her village became followers of Jesus as a result (John 4:1–42).

Just before he ascended to heaven, Jesus singled out Samaria as one of the important places for his disciples to spread the good news about him (Acts 1:8). The disciples obeyed, with Acts 8:4–25 recording how Philip brought life-changing revival to Samaria, followed by Peter and John praying for the Holy Spirit to fill the Samaritan believers, just as he had filled the Jewish disciples of Jesus (Acts 2). Acts 8:25 reports that as Peter and John traveled back to Jerusalem, "they stopped in many Samaritan villages along the way to preach the Good News." A thriving church was planted in Samaria (Acts 9:31), and Acts 15:1–3 tells of a time several years later when Paul and Barnabas stopped in Samaria to visit that very church.

Later Samaritan History

In AD 529, centuries after those first Jesus-following Samaritans, Samaria revolted against Roman rule. In response, the Roman emperor outlawed the Samaritan religion and crushed the rebellion. This included wholesale killings of Samaritans and the obliteration of their synagogues. Subsequent purges nearly wiped this people group from the face of the earth. Very few Samaritans have survived their bleak history—as of 2024, the Samaritan population numbered only about eight hundred. They are mostly located in the city of Nablus in the West Bank (next to Mount Gerizim) and in the town of Holon, near Tel Aviv/Jaffa, Israel. Samaritans still observe religious rites like the Sabbath, the Passover, and the Day of Atonement, and Mount Gerizim remains their most holy mountain.

Modern-day Samaritans celebrate the biblical feast of Shavuot on Mount Gerizim

Timeline of Samaritan History

722 BC: Assyria conquers Israel, setting the stage for intermarriage between Assyrians and Israelites and the emergence of the Samaritan people.

539 BC: Exiled Jews return to Judah, resulting in tensions with neighboring Samaritans.

500–401 BC: Samaritans build their temple on Mount Gerizim.

323–63 BC: Greek rule; Jews and Samaritans antagonize each other.

168 BC: Samaritans dedicate their temple to a Greek god, upsetting Jews.

128 BC: Jews destroy the Samaritan temple and rule Samaria.

63 BC: Romans rule Samaritans and Jews.

AD 8: Samaritans scatter bones in the Jewish temple.

AD 27–48: Jesus and his disciples minister to Samaritans.

529: The Roman emperor kills many Samaritans after they revolt.

2024: Samaritans number about 800 and continue their sacrifices and rituals.

Live It

After so many centuries, it can be easy to trivialize the circumstances and impact of the Parable of the Good Samaritan. Perhaps you've seen it delightfully illustrated in a children's book, or you've heard it preached from the pulpit, or you've glossed over it in your Bible reading. Familiarity, it seems, breeds disinterest.

The truth is, though, Jesus isn't simply calling his followers to be nice to everybody or to remember to be helpful to those they meet along the way. The actual reality of his message to "love your neighbor as yourself" (Luke 10:27) is a tough one. Based on the example of the Good Samaritan, there is always the possibility it could get messy and involve a host of people who care only about themselves.

Yet Jesus still asks us to do what he did: to step into the mess of humanity, always ready to stop and give healing and hope to those who don't deserve it, who can never repay us, and who might actually oppose us when we're trying to help them. We're called to serve with authentic compassion, no matter who it is that is in need, and even when it might hurt us financially, emotionally, or personally in some way.

Ultimately, of course, the Parable of the Good Samaritan is a sobering, frightening, fantastic reminder of the sacrificial cost that Jesus paid for our redemption. It is also a reminder of the hard possibilities we might encounter when we endeavor to authentically *love our neighbors as ourselves.*

Life Application Questions

1. Whom do you see the church treating as "a despised Samaritan" (Luke 10:33) today? What do you think should be done about that?

2. When Jesus says to you, "Go and do the same" (Luke 10:37), what emotions are stirred in you? Dread? Excitement? Fear? Joy? Explain.

3. The Samaritan in Jesus's parable does not appear to have financial limitations in regard to his actions. How might someone with limited resources follow the Samaritan's example today?

4. How would you answer the question, "Who is my neighbor?" (Luke 10:29)? List at least three names and some actions you can take to love each one "as yourself" (Luke 10:27).

NAME	ACTIONS
1.	
2.	
3.	

5. After your study of this parable, what do you want to pray about this week? Write down your thoughts, and refer to them during your prayer time each day.

Living Outside the Book

Now it's time to take your study outside of this book and into your real life. Try this: *Read a biography of Mother Teresa of Calcutta or Peter Claver of Columbia*. Both are extreme examples of a Good Samaritan lifestyle in daily practice.

- **Peter (Pedro) Claver** was a priest who lived during the 1600s. He spent the bulk of his life in what is now the South American nation of Columbia, ministering to Africans brutally enslaved by Spanish colonists. He would meet the slave ships in the harbor and go inside the filthy holds to clean and feed the frightened men and women brought in chains to the New World. Claver became known as the patron saint of the enslaved. Check your local library for the book *Street of the Half-Moon: An Account of the Spanish Noble, Pedro Claver,* by Mabel Farnum, or simply google the name *Peter Claver*.

- **Mother Teresa** lived during the twentieth century and spent most of her life in Calcutta, India. She felt called to serve the poorest of the poor, helping them to die with dignity. She was known to roam the streets of Calcutta to find the sick and dying and then physically carry them back to the home for the dying that she founded. Her ministry spread worldwide, and she became an international symbol of peace and hope. Learn more by reading *Mother Teresa: An Authorized Biography,* by Kathryn Spink, or for a quick study, read Jim Gigliotti's children's book, *Who Was Mother Teresa?* You can also google her name to discover more.

Let these two lives be an inspiration and encouragement in your own pursuit of a Good Samaritan lifestyle today.

Notes

Parables about
God's Kingdom

The Seed Parables

How would you describe an ideal kingdom? Maybe you would start by talking about majestic castles and lush, green, rolling countryside—something out of the European Middle Ages. You'd likely also mention noble kings and queens, valiant knights, brave and loyal citizens, princes and princesses performing wondrous deeds, and romantic fantasies about King Arthur's court.

Jesus, on the other hand, didn't think those kinds of grandiose descriptions were worthy of the kingdom of God (a term used interchangeably with "kingdom of heaven" in the Gospels). Instead, in Mark 4:26–32, he taught us that God's kingdom "is like" humble, tiny seeds that grow with unseen, yet unstoppable, energy. They just keep growing until they've become so much more than we could imagine if we were judging just by the tiny seed itself.

This is the mystery of God's heavenly kingdom: It appears remarkably insignificant to the human eye, yet its growth is truly unstoppable. Let's explore more about that as we dig into the Parable of the Growing Seed and the Parable of the Mustard Seed.

Read It

Key Bible Passage

For this session, read Mark 4:26–32.

Optional Reading

Explore the Parable of the Farmer Scattering Seed, the first "seed parable" Jesus told about the kingdom of God (Matt. 13:3–9, 18–23; Mark 4:3–8, 14–20; Luke 8:5–8, 11–15). More options include other accounts of the Parable of the Mustard Seed (Matt. 13:31–32; Luke 13:18–19); Jesus's comments about faith the size of a mustard seed (Matt. 17:19–20); and a conversation between Jesus and Pilate about Jesus's kingdom (John 18:28–38).

Other parables about God's kingdom (some may overlap with other types of parables):

- The Yeast (Matt. 13:33; Luke 13:20–21)
- The Hidden Treasure; The Pearl (Matt. 13:44–46)
- The Fishing Net (Matt. 13:47–52)
- The Unforgiving Debtor (Matt. 18:21–35)
- The Ten Bridesmaids (Matt. 25:1–13); The Absent Householder (Mark 13:34–37); The Watchful Servants (Luke 12:35–40)
- The Three Servants (Matt. 25:14–30); The Ten Servants (Luke 19:11–27)

> The Kingdom of God is like a farmer who scatters seed on the ground.
>
> MARK 4:26

Know It

1. Based on the descriptions in these parables, how would you describe the kingdom of God in your own words?

2. The Parable of the Growing Seed mentions three symbolic aspects of God's constantly growing kingdom: "a leaf blade," "heads of wheat," and ripened grain (Mark 4:28). What would you guess each of these represents?

3. The Parable of the Mustard Seed also mentions three symbolic elements of God's kingdom: It has "long branches," it provides "shade," and it attracts nesting "birds" (Mark 4:32). What do you think each of these represents?

Jesus Teaches with Authority

The Gospel writers report that crowds were "amazed" ("astonished" in the KJV) at Jesus's teaching—not so much over what he said, but *how* he said it. Mark 1:22 describes it this way: "The people were amazed at his teaching, for he taught with real authority—quite unlike the teachers of religious law" (see also Matt. 7:28–29; Luke 4:32).

This kind of authoritative instruction is evident in the two parables of growing seeds that Jesus told in Mark 4:26–32. Even reading this passage today, you get the feeling that he's not just laying out theories about the kingdom of God, but that Jesus is speaking from personal experience with God's heavenly kingdom. The way he talks, with *authority*, communicates a "been there, done that" kind of knowledge that he was sharing with anyone who had ears willing to hear.

Jesus's divine, intimate expertise with heaven and eternity influenced the very first sermons he preached, even before he had called his original disciples. Mark 1:14–15 reports he went through Galilee proclaiming the same world-changing idea: "The Kingdom of God is near!" This was a repeated theme in his teaching and a message he instructed his disciples to spread as well (see, for example, Matt. 4:17; 10:7; 11:12; 12:28; Luke 8:1; 9:2, 11; 10:9; 11:20; 17:21).

What Is God's Kingdom?

As his earthly ministry progressed, Jesus began expanding on this lesson for his hearers, providing parables and comparisons to describe what God's heavenly kingdom "is like." For instance:

- "The Kingdom of Heaven is like a treasure that a man discovered hidden in a field." (Matt. 13:44)

- "The Kingdom of Heaven is like a merchant on the lookout for choice pearls." (Matt. 13:45)
- "The Kingdom of Heaven is like a fishing net that was thrown into the water and caught fish of every kind." (Matt. 13:47)
- "The Kingdom of Heaven can be compared to a king who decided to bring his accounts up to date with servants who had borrowed money from him." (Matt. 18:23)
- "What else is the Kingdom of God like? It is like the yeast a woman used in making bread." (Luke 13:20–21)

Jesus employed this same kind of comparative teaching technique when he told the parables of The Growing Seed and The Mustard Seed. People had come to hear Jesus teach as he stood on the northern shore of the Sea of Galilee. Then more people came, and even more, until the whole beach was packed and there was barely room left for the Teacher! Rather than dismiss the crowd and send them home, Mark tells us, "He got into a boat. Then he sat in the boat while all the people remained on the shore. He taught them by telling many stories in the form of parables" (Mark 4:1–2).

Aerial view of the Bay of Parables, on the Sea of Galilee

Today, that place where Jesus sat in the boat is called the Bay of Parables, in honor of Jesus's teaching on that ancient day. Here is one description of it: "A lovely little cove ... the topography around the bay creates a natural amphitheater with the land sloping gently up to where grass and wildflowers grow in springtime. According to tests conducted by an archaeologist and a sound engineer, a single orator standing in a boat anchored offshore could be heard clearly by an audience of several thousand."[17]

It was most likely in this cove that Jesus turned his attention again to the question, What is the kingdom of heaven *like*? The answer, according to him, was seen in the example of a seed. The first seed parable that Jesus tells in the bay is about a farmer who scattered seed among different kinds of soil (Mark 4:1–9). Then, after an interlude that tells how the disciples discover the meaning of that parable and the importance of listening to Jesus's teaching (Mark 4:10–25), Jesus tells two other seed parables: the Parable of the Growing Seed and the Parable of the Mustard Seed (Mark 4:26–32).

Parable of the Growing Seed

In the Parable of the Growing Seed (Mark 4:26–29), Jesus points to the miracle of the unseen vibrancy as a "seed sprouts and grows." The farmer doesn't understand exactly how that happens, but he reaps the windfall of a harvest anyway. Some believe this parable is actually a continuation or expanded explanation of the Parable of the Farmer Scattering Seed recorded in Mark 4:1–9, which is possible, although it can stand on its own without needing the previous parable to justify it.

Regardless, it's interesting that to describe the kingdom of God, Jesus chose the common imagery of farming, which people living in that ancient time could easily relate to. Notably, as New Testament scholars N. T. Wright and Michael Bird remind us, in this farming context, Jesus "does not refer to 'heaven' as the final post-mortem destination of God's people but to the arrival of God's sovereign, saving, 'heavenly' rule on earth itself."[18] And, according to Jesus, the ongoing arrival of that "'heavenly' rule on earth" is quite like seeds of grain that are scattered by a farmer.

In Jesus's time, after the first rain of winter, a farmer typically planted wheat seed (or other grain seed) by pouring seeds into a makeshift pouch created by turning up the front of his cloak, then walking along tossing seed here and there so it would germinate in the ground. At that point, the miracle of God would take over, leaving the farmer only to watch and hope. Jesus explained, "Night and day, while [the farmer is] asleep or awake, the seed sprouts and grows, but he does not understand how it happens. The earth produces the crops on its own" (Mark 4:27–28).

The key phrase in this parable is in verse 28: "on its own" or "all by itself" (NIV). In the original Greek text of Mark's Gospel, that phrase is actually just one word, *automate*, which is based on the root word *automatos*. Our modern adaptation of that word is "automatic," which stays pretty close to the ancient meaning of *automatos*: "of its own accord." In other words, Jesus seems to be saying, there's nothing anyone can do to make God's kingdom grow in our world or to speed up its spreading influence—and nothing anyone can do to stop it either. This is a hard truth for many of us today, as it would have also been for some of Jesus's original audience. We prefer to take responsibility for our own success—including the spread of God's kingdom here on earth—but this parable doesn't give us that option. That's actually a good thing because, as scholar Mark Bailey says, "By its very nature the kingdom will succeed because *God alone is responsible for its success*" (emphasis added).[19]

Crops growing in central Israel

Understanding the Parable of the Growing Seed

This parable has generated quite a few ideas about how it should be understood. Which seems most likely to you?

1. Early Christian leaders viewed it as a description of how God's kingdom gradually transforms civilizations.
2. In Medieval times, it represented God redeeming human hearts (planting the seed), the seed growing through the efforts of Christian workers, and the seed maturing for the final day of judgment (the harvest).
3. Some see this parable depicting only the situation at the time Jesus told it, relating the story to Jesus's statement that "the harvest is great, but the workers are few" (Matt. 9:37).
4. One popular interpretation is that Jesus used this story to give a warning about the nearness of God's final judgment, when he "harvests it [people] with a sickle" (Mark 4:29).
5. Some think that Jesus told this parable to address the impatience of those who thought Jesus's ministry should be accomplishing more to thwart their Roman oppressors.
6. Many view this parable as a reminder that God's kingdom grows because of his miraculous touch, not because of any "good works" that people do.
7. Some see this parable as a demonstration of God's grace to sinners—that he continues to allow more time for the news of his kingdom to spread because "he does not want anyone to be destroyed" (2 Peter 3:9).[20]

Parable of the Mustard Seed

In Jesus's next seed parable (Mark 4:30–32), he uses the object lesson of a mustard seed—one of the tiniest seeds in the world—that eventually grows into an enormous plant. As with the Parable of the Growing Seed, we discover a few interesting elements if we take a look at the cultural background of this story.

First, we know today that the mustard seed is not actually "the smallest of all seeds" (Mark 4:31), as Jesus told his audience. The cypress seed is smaller, as is an orchid seed. Some argue that this means Jesus was fallible and that he made a mistake in scientific knowledge. However, this view ignores the context of his farming parables in Mark 4, which use for examples the seeds that farmers used to grow food in ancient Israel. In that farming environment and at that time, the mustard seed was indeed the smallest known seed that was regularly cultivated, and it later even became a proverbial prototype for smallness in Jewish wisdom literature.

Tiny black mustard seeds

Because of its smallness and wide use in ancient times, the seed Jesus spoke of in this parable is identified by most Bible historians as the black mustard seed (*Brassica nigra*). That seed is so tiny that you can fit hundreds of them in the palm of your hand. Despite the seed's minuscule size, the black mustard plant can actually grow to be as tall as a modern-day basketball goal—8–10 feet high.[21] In Jesus's day, *Brassica nigra* was also a multipurpose seed: Farmers used it to grow crops, and the seed itself was also ground into powder or made into paste for use as a topical medicine, as well as for spicing foods.[22]

In addition to comparing the kingdom of God to the astonishing growth pent up inside a tiny mustard seed, Jesus made one final comment in this parable that's had theologians arguing for centuries: "Birds can make nests in its shade" (Mark 4:32). It's possible, of course, that this reference to birds inhabiting the symbolic kingdom of God is just that—a reference to birds. But some symbologists look to Ezekiel 17:22–23 and Daniel 4:10–12 in the Old Testament and see more. With that backdrop, they believe Mark 4:32 is a symbolic promise from Jesus that non-Jews (gentiles) from the world over will also find an eternal home in God's grace-filled kingdom.

Despite the fascinating imagery and cultural background of both seed parables, Jesus's message and focus remains the same: The influence of God's heavenly kingdom is relentlessly growing throughout our world, whether or not we can see it and regardless of whether or not we even believe it. And that growth can never be stopped—no matter what.

Wild black mustard plants

Live It

It's interesting that Jesus never said, "The kingdom of God is ..." but instead always said, "The kingdom of God *is like* ..." He could have simply given us a definition or a clear explanation of what this kingdom is, and how we can identify it and classify it without confusion. But he didn't do that; his descriptions of God's kingdom are always symbolic and therefore frustratingly vague. They are also (as history has proven) open to multiple, sometimes conflicting, and often confusing interpretations.

At the same time, Jesus never suggested that this kingdom of heaven was some abstract, immaterial thing. His frequent message is that God's kingdom not only exists but is also a present, undeniable reality—and that it continues to expand throughout our world. As of today, it's been growing for a minimum of two thousand years or so.

These truths raise some difficult questions in regard to practical Christian living. How are we supposed to recognize and interact with God's present, real, yet invisible kingdom in our world today? Why hasn't the unstoppable expansion of God's kingdom made more of a difference in our harsh, sinful world? Why does the kingdom of God on earth *matter*, here where sin seems to reign supreme in everyday life?

Jesus, it seems, was unwilling to give easy answers to those kinds of questions, preferring instead to give only clues through parables like those found in Mark 4:26–32. And perhaps that's the point: Here in a world where sin, cruelty, war, and unkindness do seem to reign supreme, we who follow Jesus can still cling to hope because—in spite of everything—the kingdom of God on earth refuses to retreat. It cannot and will not go away. Like a growing seed, night and day it sprouts and grows, even though we don't understand how it happens. This is a wondrous hope we hold for each new day—a hope that can never be taken away.

Life Application Questions

1. Of these two parables, do you have a favorite? If so, why?

2. John 18:36 records Jesus saying, "My Kingdom is not of this world." How does this influence your understanding of the Parable of the Growing Seed and the Parable of the Mustard Seed?

3. In what ways have you noticed the growth of God's kingdom in your own life and surroundings?

4. In what ways has the kingdom of God provided you with "shade" (Mark 4:32) and shelter?

5. What is the most important thing you want to remember from your study of these two parables? In what ways do their messages give you hope or change the way you will approach your life going forward?

Living Outside the Book

Now it's time to take your study outside of this book and into your real life. Try this: *Create a physical reminder of the invisible presence of God's always-growing kingdom by growing a black mustard plant in your home.*

First, buy a package of black mustard seeds—the kind used for planting. You can find these online year-round or at your local garden center during the spring and summer. You'll want to start your mustard plant in a pot that is at least six inches deep (a one-gallon pot is recommended), and it should contain drainage holes.

Fill your pot two-thirds or so with good potting soil, then sprinkle the mustard seeds across the top. Hand-press the seeds into the dirt, then add another thin layer of soil over them. Water the seeds, but be careful not to overwater, which can cause fungus. Place the pot near a window where it can receive partial to full sunlight. Water regularly and add organic fertilizer if desired.

When the plant grows large enough and the weather warm enough, transfer the plant to an ideal spot in the ground outside. Mustard plants are annuals, not perennials, so if you like this project, make plans to do it again every year!

Every time you see and care for this black mustard seed plant, let it remind you of Mark 4:26–32 and the hope we have in the growth of God's kingdom on earth.

Notes

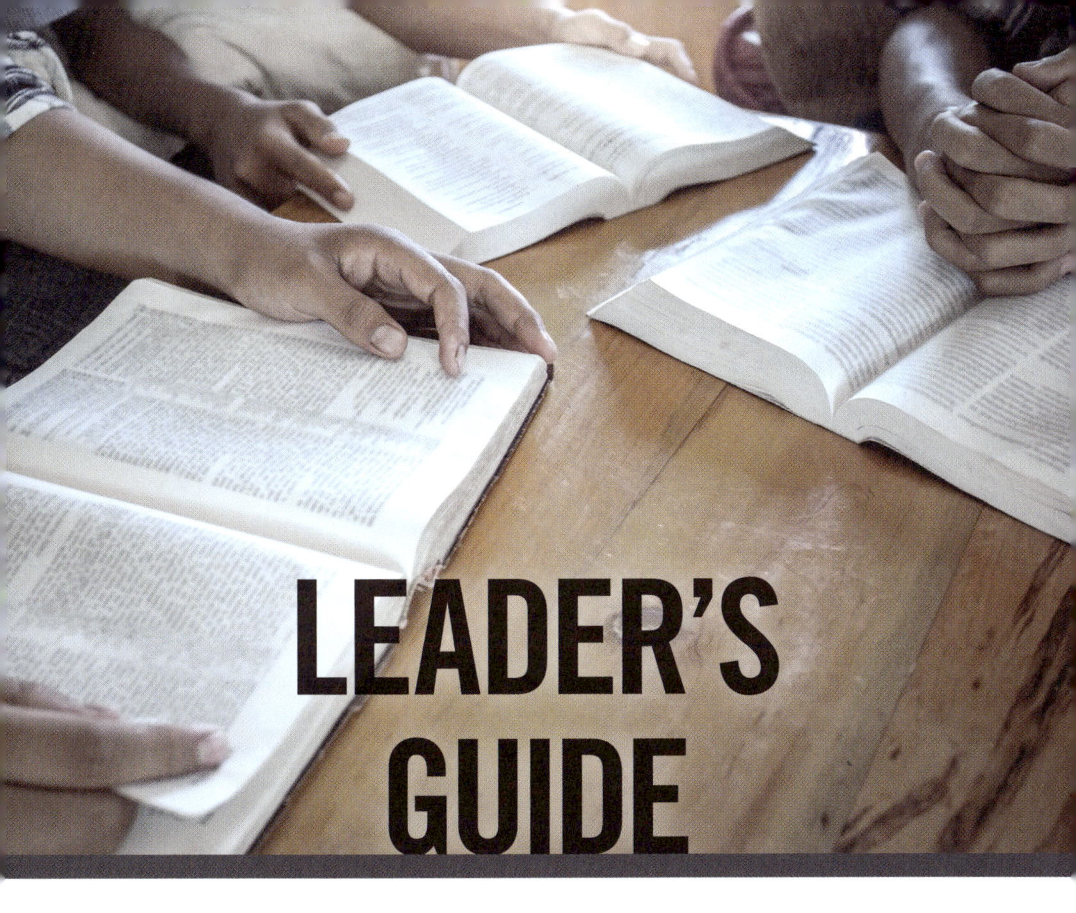

"Encourage one another and build each other up."

1 THESSALONIANS 5:11

Leader's Guide

Congratulations! You've either decided to lead a Bible study, or you're thinking hard about it. Guess what? God does big things through small groups. When his people gather together, open his Word, and invite his Spirit to work, their lives are changed!

Do you feel intimidated yet?

Be comforted by this: even the great apostle Paul felt "in over his head" at times. When he went to Corinth to help people grasp God's truth, he admitted he was overwhelmed: "I came to you in weakness with great fear and trembling" (1 Corinthians 2:3). Later he wondered, "Who is adequate for such a task as this?" (2 Corinthians 2:16 NLT).

Feelings of inadequacy are normal; every leader has them. What's more, they're actually healthy. They keep us dependent on the Lord. It is in our times of greatest weakness that God works most powerfully. The Lord assured Paul, "My grace is sufficient for you, for my power is made perfect in weakness" (2 Corinthians 12:9).

The Goal

What is the goal of a Bible study group? Listen as the apostle Paul speaks to Christians:

- "Oh, my dear children! I feel as if I'm going through labor pains for you again, and they will continue until *Christ is fully developed in your lives*" (Galatians 4:19 NLT, emphasis added).
- "For God knew his people in advance, and he chose them *to become like his Son*" (Romans 8:29 NLT, emphasis added).

Do you see it? God's ultimate goal for us is that we would become like Jesus Christ. This means a Bible study is not about filling our heads with more information. Rather, it is about undergoing transformation. We study and apply God's truth so that it will reshape our hearts and minds, and so that over time, we will become more and more like Jesus.

Paul said, "The purpose of my instruction is that all believers would be filled with love that comes from a pure heart, a clear conscience, and genuine faith" (1 Timothy 1:5 NLT).

This isn't about trying to "master the Bible." No, we're praying that God's Word will master us, and through humble submission to its authority, we'll be changed from the inside out.

Your Role

Many group leaders experience frustration because they confuse their role with God's role. Here's the truth: God alone knows our deep hang-ups and hurts. Only he can save a soul, heal a heart, fix a life. It is God who rescues people from depression, addictions, bitterness, guilt, and shame. We Bible study leaders need to realize that *we can't do any of those things.*

So what can we do? More than we think!

- We can pray.
- We can trust God to work powerfully.
- We can obey the Spirit's promptings.
- We can prepare for group gatherings.
- We can keep showing up faithfully.

With group members:

- We can invite, remind, encourage, and love.
- We can ask good questions and then listen attentively.
- We can gently speak tough truths.
- We can celebrate with those who are happy and weep with those who are sad.
- We can call and text and let them know we've got their back.

But we can never do the things that only the Almighty can do.

- We can't play the Holy Spirit in another person's life.
- We can't be in charge of outcomes.
- We can't force God to work according to our timetables.

And one more important reminder: besides God's role and our role, group members also have a key role to play in this process. If they don't show up, prepare, or open their hearts to God's transforming truth, no life change will take place. We're not called to manipulate or shame, pressure or arm twist. We're not to blame if members don't make progress—and we don't get the credit when they do. We're mere instruments in the hands of God.

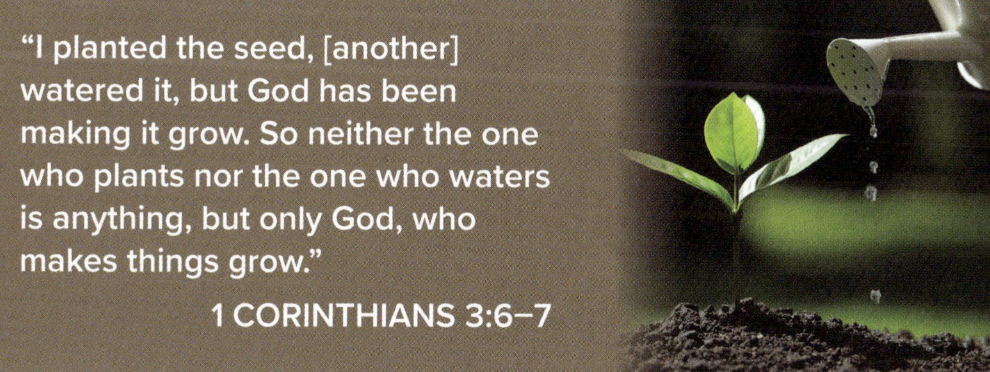

Leader Myths and Truths

Many people assume that a Bible study leader should:

- Be a Bible scholar.
- Be a dynamic communicator.
- Have a big, fancy house to meet in.
- Have it all together—no doubts, bad habits, or struggles.

These are myths—even outright lies of the enemy!

Here's the truth:

- God is looking for humble Bible students, not scholars.
- You're not signing up to give lectures, you're agreeing to facilitate discussions.
- You don't need a palace, just a place where you can have uninterrupted discussions. (Perhaps one of your group members will agree to host your study.)
- Nobody has it all together. We are all in process. We are all seeking to work out "our salvation with fear and trembling" (Philippians 2:12).

As long as your desire is that Jesus be Lord of your life, God will use you!

Some Bad Reasons to Lead a Group

- You want to wow others with your biblical knowledge.

  "Love . . . does not boast, it is not proud" (1 Corinthians 13:4).

- You're seeking a hidden personal gain or profit.

  "We do not peddle the word of God for profit" (2 Corinthians 2:17).

- You want to tell people how wrong they are.

  "Do not condemn" (Romans 2:1).

- You want to fix or rescue people.

  "It is God who works in you to will and to act" (Philippians 2:13).

- You're being pressured to do it.

  "Am I now trying to win the approval of human beings, or of God?" (Galatians 1:10).

A Few Do's

✔ Pray for your group.

Are you praying for your group members regularly? It is the most important thing a leader can do for his or her group.

✔ Ask for help.

If you're new at leading, spend time with an experienced group leader and pick his or her brain.

✔ Encourage members to prepare.

Challenge participants to read the Bible passages and the material in their study guides, and to answer and reflect on the study questions during the week prior to meeting.

✔ Discuss the group guidelines.

Go over important guidelines with your group at the first session, and again as needed if new members join the group in later sessions. See the *Group Guidelines* at the end of this leader's guide.

✔ Share the load.

Don't be a one-person show. Ask for volunteers. Let group members host the meeting, arrange for snacks, plan socials, lead group prayer times, and so forth. The old saying is true: Participants become boosters; spectators become critics.

✔ Be flexible.

If a group member shows up in crisis, it is okay to stop and take time to surround the hurting brother or sister with love. Provide a safe place for sharing. Listen and pray for his or her needs.

✔ Be kind.

Remember, there's a story—often a heart-breaking one—behind every face. This doesn't *excuse* bad or disruptive behavior on the part of group members, but it might *explain* it.

A Few Don'ts

✘ Don't "wing it."

Although these sessions are designed to require minimum preparation, read each one ahead of time. Highlight the questions you feel are especially important for your group to spend time on.

✘ Don't feel ashamed to say, "I don't know."

Disciple means "learner," not "know-it-all."

✘ Don't feel the need to "dump the truck."

You don't have to say everything you know. There is always next week. A little silence during group discussion time, that's fine. Let members wrestle with questions.

✘ Don't put members on the spot.

Invite others to share and pray, but don't pressure them. Give everyone an opportunity to participate. People will open up on their own time as they learn to trust the group.

✘ Don't go down "rabbit trails."

Be careful not to let one person dominate the time or for the discussion to go down the gossip road. At the same time, don't short-circuit those occasions when the Holy Spirit is working in your group members' lives and therefore they *need* to share a lot.

✘ Don't feel pressure to cover every question.

Better to have a robust discussion of four questions than a superficial conversation of ten.

✘ Don't go long.

Encourage good discussion, but don't be afraid to "rope 'em back in" when needed. Start and end on time. If you do this from the beginning, you'll avoid the tendency of group members to arrive later and later as the season goes on.

How to Use This Study Guide

Many group members have busy lives—dealing with long work hours, childcare, and a host of other obligations. These sessions are designed to be as simple and straightforward as possible to fit into a busy schedule. Nevertheless, encourage group members to set aside some time during the week (even if it's only a little) to pray, read the key Bible passage, and respond to questions in this study guide. This will make the group discussion and experience much more rewarding for everyone.

Each session contains four parts.

Read It

The *Key Bible Passage* is the portion of Scripture everyone should read during the week before the group meeting. The group can read it together at the beginning of the session as well.

The *Optional Reading* is for those who want to dig deeper and read lengthier Bible passages on their own during the week.

Know It

This section encourages participants to reflect on the Bible passage they've just read. Here, the goal is to interact with the biblical text and grasp what it says. (We'll get into practical application later.)

Explore It

Here group members can find background information with charts and visuals to help them understand the Bible passage and the topic more deeply. They'll move beyond the text itself and see how it connects to other parts of Scripture and the historical and cultural context.

Live It

Finally, participants will examine how God's Word connects to their lives. There are application questions for group discussion or personal reflection, practical ideas to apply what they've learned from God's Word, and a closing thought and/or prayer. (Remember, you don't have to cover all the questions or everything in this section during group time. Focus on what's most important for your group.)

Celebrate!

Here's an idea: Have a plan for celebrating your time together after the last session of this Bible study. Do something special after your gathering time, or plan a separate celebration for another time and place. Maybe someone in your group has the gift of hospitality—let them use their gifting and organize the celebration.

	30-MINUTE SESSION	60-MINUTE SESSION
READ IT	Open in prayer and read the *Key Bible Passage.* 5 minutes	Open in prayer and read the *Key Bible Passage.* 5 minutes
KNOW IT	Ask: "What stood out to you from this Bible passage?" 5 minutes	Ask: "What stood out to you from this Bible passage?" 5 minutes
EXPLORE IT	Encourage group members to read this section on their own, but don't spend group time on it. Move on to the life application questions.	Ask: "What did you find new or helpful in the *Explore It* section? What do you still have questions about?" 10 minutes
LIVE IT	Members voluntarily share their answers to 3 or 4 of the life application questions. 15 minutes	Members voluntarily share their answers to the life application questions. 25 minutes
PRAYER & CLOSING	Conclude with a brief prayer. 5 minutes	Share prayer requests and praise reports. Encourage the group to pray for each other in the coming week. Conclude with a brief prayer. 15 minutes

	90-MINUTE SESSION
	Open in prayer and read the *Key Bible Passage.* 5 minutes
	• Ask: "What stood out to you from this Bible passage?" • Then go over the *Know It* questions as a group. 10 minutes
	• Ask: "What did you find new or helpful in the *Explore It* section? What do you still have questions about?" • Here, the leader can add information found while preparing for the session. • If there are questions or a worksheet in this section, go over those as a group. 20 minutes
	• Members voluntarily share their answers to the life application questions. • Wrap up this time with a closing thought or suggestions for how to put into practice in the coming week what was just learned from God's Word. 30 minutes
	• Share prayer requests and praise reports. • Members voluntarily pray during group time about the requests and praises shared. • Encourage the group to pray for each other in the coming week. 25 minutes

Group Guidelines

This group is about discovering God's truth, supporting each other, and finding growth in our new life in Christ. To reach these goals, a group needs a few simple guidelines that everyone should follow for the group to stay healthy and for trust to develop.

1. **Everyone agrees to make group time a priority.**
   We understand that there are work, health, and family issues that come up. So if there is an emergency or schedule conflict that cannot be avoided, be sure to let someone know that you can't make it that week. This may seem like a small thing, but it makes a big difference to your other group members.

2. **What is said in the group stays in the group.**
   Accept it now: we are going to share some personal things. Therefore, the group must be a safe and confidential place to share.

3. **Don't be judgmental, even if you strongly disagree.**
   Listen first, and contribute your perspective only as needed. Remember, you don't fully know someone else's story. Take this advice from James: "Be quick to listen, slow to speak, and slow to become angry" (James 1:19).

4. **Be patient with one another.**
   We are all in process, and some of us are hurting and struggling more than others. Don't expect bad habits or attitudes to disappear overnight.

5. **Everyone participates.**
   It may take time to learn how to share, but as you develop a trust toward the other group members, take the chance.

If you struggle in any of these areas, ask God's help for growth, and ask the group to help hold you accountable. Remember, you're all growing together.

Notes

1 Reader's Digest, *Complete Guide to the Bible* (The Reader's Digest Association, 1998), 318.

2 Klyne R. Snodgrass, *Stories with Intent*, 2nd ed. (William B. Eerdmans, 2018), 2.

3 Herbert Lockyer, *All the Parables of the Bible* (Zondervan, 1963), 11–12.

4 Larry Richards, *Every Teaching of Jesus in the Bible* (Thomas Nelson, 2001), 62.

5 Richards, *Every Teaching of Jesus in the Bible*, 63–64. Richards's view does raise a question about when it is actually too late for a sinner to be redeemed, especially if that sinner is still living. But that's a much more complicated question best reserved for a different book.

6 Millard J. Erickson, *Christian Theology*, 3rd ed. (Baker Academic, 2013), 857.

7 Dr. Timothy Paul Jones, interview by the author, January 20, 2024.

8 Ted Cabal, ed., *The Apologetics Study Bible* (Holman Bible Publishers, 2007), 1450.

9 Mark Strauss, *Zondervan Illustrated Bible Backgrounds Commentary*, ed. Clinton E. Arnold, vol. 1 (Zondervan, 2002), 446.

10 Dmitri Royster, *The Parables* (St. Vladimir's Seminary Press, 1996), 75.

11 Craig S. Keener, *The IVP Bible Background Commentary: New Testament* (InterVarsity Press, 1993), 231–32.

12 Strauss, *Zondervan Illustrated Bible Backgrounds Commentary*, vol. 1, 446.

13 John A. Beck, *A Walking Tour of the Gospels* (Our Daily Bread Publishing, 2023), 209.

14 Albert Barnes, *Notes on the New Testament: Luke and John* (Baker Book House, 1980), 103.

15 Strauss, *Zondervan Illustrated Bible Backgrounds Commentary*, vol. 1, 448.

16 Craig L. Blomberg, *Interpreting the Parables*, 2nd ed. (IVP Academic, 2002), 295–96.

17 Charles R. Swindoll, *Swindoll's Living Insights New Testament Commentary: Mark* (Tyndale, 2016), 109.

18 N. T. Wright and Michael Bird, *The New Testament in Its World* (Zondervan Academic, 2019), 595.

19 Mark Bailey and Tom Constable, *The New Testament Explorer* (Word Publishing, 1999), 75.

20 The information in this section is gleaned from Snodgrass, *Stories with Intent*, 183–84.

21 Amy-Jill Levine, *Short Stories by Jesus* (HarperOne, 2015), 170.

22 Merrill C. Tenney and J. D. Douglas, eds., *The New International Dictionary of the Bible*, pictorial ed. (Regnery Reference Library, 1987), 801.